MY THOUGHTS

By

Larry Hint

DEDICATION

To Ginny Hint, my faithful wife, partner, and friend.

Thank you.

FOREWARD

By Roberta Baker

We at the Allentown United Methodist have enjoyed Larry's "Words of Wisdom". We love and appreciate Larry because he gives so much of himself and is always willing to give a helping hand, a loving hug, and a piece of candy to the little ones. It is a blessing to have him and his wife Ginny in our congregation.

Praise the Lord!

Praise the Lord for creating an egg in the womb.

For giving it life and making it grow.

Praise the Lord for breath when babies are born.

Praise the Lord for watching over children while they are growing.

Praise the Lord for watching over all of us as we go through life with angels for protection.

Praise the Lord for taking us back home at the end of our lives.

Praise the Lord!

Amazing Grace

Amazing is the power of the Lord that reaches the far corners of the earth.

Amazing is the pardon the Lord offers to all of us.

Amazing is the mercy the Lord shows to all His people.

Amazing is the love He gives to all.

Amazing Grace how sweet the sound, that saved a retch like me.

Have you been saved?

Amazing Grace

In the Arms of an Angel

In the arms of an angel, what a wonderful place to be.

The angels protect us from all harm and keep us safe.

The angels' wings carry us to new heights where we could not go without them.

The angels guide us every day, in everything we do and watch over us until eternity.

How Big is God

God is bigger than the universe.
He is everywhere.
He is in our hearts with love that is bigger than the outdoors.
He is in our souls.
He is in our minds.
He is in our bodies.
He is in every day of our lives.
That is how big God is.

911

Where in the world were you, when the world
stopped turning, on that September day?

Were you in bed, covering your head, afraid to come
out?

Or were you driving your car with the radio on, and
couldn't believe what you were hearing? Were you
so shocked that you almost drove into a ditch?

Were you at home with the TV on, and couldn't
believe your eyes?

Did you see the second plane fly into the towers?

Did you bow your head and pray to God to stop
all this tragedy?

Did you go to church and pray really hard
for all the people and their families?

Or were you at work running a turret lathe and you
just wanted to stop the machine and cry? Where
were you when the world stopped turning?

The Mind is a Terrible Thing to Waste

The mind is a terrible thing to waste.
We should use it to think of nice things to do for
friends and relatives.
We should use it to help make peace in the world.
We should use it to better our way of life.
We should not use it to be greedy or selfish and hurt
other people.
A little bit of kindness goes a long way to make a
peaceful world.
Peace on earth, good will toward men.

We Can Change Things

There are things that we can say and there are things
that we can do, for ourselves and for the Lord.
We can change the way we feel about religion and
the way we pray.
We can pray for all the people that don't believe.
We can pray for all the people that need us.
We can change things.

The Lord Will Never Let You Down

The Lord will never let you down.
He is always there around to protect you, to comfort
you, to bless you and to love you. Like He loved His
Son.
He is there in our mind. He is there in our hearts.
He is there in our soul, and He will be there forever.

The Prayers of a Common Man

I went to the Lord several times in my life to pray for
major concerns.
I prayed to get through boot camp, I prayed to make
it safely through the "Cuban Crises."
I prayed that I would make it through a hurricane,
while on a ship in the Atlantic.
I prayed when I had colon cancer.
But the prayers of a common man are the prayers
you pray each day. You pray for the health and
safety of your children and grandchildren, and that
you will live to see them grown. And you thank God
for all the blessings you have in your life.

Jesus Take My Hand

Jesus take my hand and lead me, guide me and pray for me.
Lead me through the valley of the shadow of death.
Thou art with me.
Protect me.
Jesus, take me home.

OVER THE RAINBOW

Over the rainbow way up high is one of God's greatest creations.
Everyone looks for the pot of gold at the end of the rainbow, but actually God put the pot of gold in your heart.
The rainbow is God's promise that He will never destroy living creatures like He did in the great flood.
The rainbow is His promise at the end of the storm.

It's a Pretty Day

In the dawn of the day, when it gets light, and God is
light. He gives us light and hope for a new day.
Beautiful blue sky all morning, a passing little
shower in the afternoon with a God-made rainbow
at its end, then blue sky again.
A bright red sky in the evening means another
pretty day tomorrow.

I Adore You

I adore you Lord for the way You talk to me as
You blow soft winds through the pine trees.
I adore you for bright sunshine days and full moon
nights.
I adore You for flowers and green grass and trees.
I adore You for spring showers and rainbows.
I thank You for giving me guidance on my path of
life.
I adore You for your one and only Son that gave
His life for my sins.
I surely do adore You.

PASSION

The passion that we have for our Lord and His only
Son Jesus.
The passion that we have for our siblings,
The passion that we have for our children and
spouse,
And also our church family, and the passion we
express for the families of flight 3407 plane crash, is
not as large as the passion our
Lord has for us His children.

Walk With Jesus

To walk with Jesus, what a wonderful thought.
What a great privilege this will be.
I will be so very proud to walk with Jesus.
I am looking forward to this.
If I keep believing in Him this will happen.
It will happen for all who believe.

Jason Dunham

Why did he do what he did? Why did he jump on a live grenade and save the lives of his fellow marines?
Was it because he was a very nice young man, and wanted to save their lives? He was so unselfish with his life. Now he is an American hero. His picture is in the Marine Core Museum in Quantico, VA. There is now a ship with his name on it, the USS Jason Dunham DDG-109. We pray that the ship lives up to his name.

To Have A Dream

To fulfill a dream is a passion you have in your life. To have children we are proud of is an answer to a perfect dream. To have dreams and goals to shoot for and make their dreams come true. To have a dream of a long and wonderful life. To dream that our children love us as much as we love them. To have a dream that Jesus will stand by us and be with us always.

STAND BY ME

It is so great to have a partner that stands by you, through thick or thin, richer or poorer, in sickness or health, to have a wife that stands by me. It is so wonderful to have the Good Lord stand by us every day of our lives. He is there with praise and love. He watches over us with angels for our protection. The Lord really does stand by me.

THE HONOR

It's an honor to obey the law of the land. It's an honor to march in a Memorial Day parade. It's an honor to meet and talk with all the military men in the parade. It's an honor to hear the speeches they make in the Memorial Day ceremony. It's a great honor just to be there. It's a great honor to serve our country. But the best honor of all is to know the parents of Jason Dunham, a real American Hero.

IN MY EYES

In my eyes the world could be much better, if we all believed in Jesus. In my eyes and in your smile the world be a happier place for all of us. In my eyes and in my mind we could think of ways to greet people and make them all happier. In my eyes we could make the world a more peaceful place to live.

The Christening of a Ship

There are a whole lot of things that go into the building of a ship.
The planning, the blueprints, the ordering of materials, the layout, the welding, the wiring, the plumbing, the painting, the hard work, and the sweat.
There are a whole lot more things that go into the naming of a ship.
The years of growing up, the love, the patience, the good times, the kindness, the memories, the trust, the heartache, the hurt, the missing, the praying, and with God's help, the healing, the love and the honor.
It all makes a wonderful ship.

Fathers' Day 2009

To be a good father takes a lot of time and patience
and a lot of kindness and love.
I had to learn that I had to be their good friend
along with being their father.
I am proud of my children and they have made me
proud to be their father.
I take my sons and grandchildren fishing and hunting
and we all have a good time together.
I know that God my Father is looking over all of us
and protects us every day of the year.
It is an honor to be a father.

The Legacy

You are the legacy that you leave. You leave a
legacy by the way you teach your children. You
teach them how to behave, to be honest, to be caring,
to work hard, to tell the truth, to help other people, to
believe in themselves, to be a good leader, to care for
other people, to love others, to have a good sense of
humor, to be a good role model, to go to church and
believe in God.

When Jesus Comes

I want to be ready when Jesus comes.
I want to be here and greet Him.
I want to see Him and talk to Him.
I want to be ready to go with Him.
I want my family and friends to be
ready for Jesus, too.
I am looking forward to be with Him.
I know Jesus loves me and will take
care of us forever.

Jesus is Real

Jesus is coming someday soon to judge us.
He will judge each and every one of us.
Jesus possesses miraculous power.
He can find us even if we hide.
He will find us and judge us.
We had better get our lives in order and confess our
sins.
We have to be ready for Him because He is real.

He Touched Me

The Lord is touching me in a way through my mind and to put these thoughts on paper.

He is teaching me faith and to trust in Him. He is a very good teacher. He can teach everyone faith and love.

All we have to do is let Him do this and it will work.

He touched my heart by the way He performs miracles and heals people. He touched my soul and tells me that I will be with Him someday. He touched me.

Lord, You Gave Me a Mountain

If my time on earth is done and tomorrow never comes, then save my soul my Savior God to thee. I surely love it here, this land was made for you and me. I am going to wait for the midnight hour, but this time, Lord, you gave me a mountain. A mountain you know I may never climb. It isn't just a hill any longer, you gave me a mountain this time.

The Woods

What a great place to see and study God's creations.

He created the ground, the hills, the trees, the streams, and the whole earth.

He created all the little critters and creatures and all the big animals of the woods.

He created the wind that talks to us as it blows through the trees.

He created all the birds that talk to us as they go on in their life.

He created the sky, the clouds, the rain, and the wonderful rainbows.

He created you and me and all our children.
God is the Master of creation.
The Holy Spirit is talking to you through me.

Our Father Who Art in Heaven

Our Father, Lord, if you kept records of our sins, then who could stand?

With you there is forgiveness for all who sin.

Put your hope in the Father, for our Father has unfailing love for all of us.

Our Father is, my Father, my fathers' father and my grandfather's father. He loves us all the same.

He watches over all of us, day and night, 24-7, year after year. He is there for us all the time.

So let's keep the peace so we can have "Peace on earth."

Reaching Out

Reaching out, touching hands, reaching for the Lord.
Reaching out, touching hands, touching me.
The Lord is reaching out for us with faith, hope, and love.
He is touching me with faith.
He is reaching out, touching me, touching you.
The Lord is reaching out to you through my thoughts in my writing.

LIFE

Life to me is a lot of uncertainty, it means a lot of hardships and a lot of hard work for very little. The one thing that holds you together is the Lord's helping hand.
He is there with you to hold you together through the rough times.
He helps you when you are down and out.
He is there to bless you for the little things and the big things that you do.
He supports you in many ways. And we do not know this until after something happens.

The Life Saver

After I read about Dr. Al-Humadi in the Olean
Times Herald, I had thoughts about how I wanted to
thank him for saving my life.

In April of 1984 he operated on me and removed a
cancer tumor and part of my colon.

Without this operation I would not have lived very
long.

At that time I had 3 sons, ages 4, 9, and 12. So you
see he gave me a new chance at life, to enjoy my
sons and their children.

He sure is a life saver.

It is an honor and a privilege to call him my doctor.

And we all thank him very much.

I'll Be There

When the weather is rough and things really get
tough, I'll be there.
When the heavens and God calls and I have done it
all, I'll be there.
When my time on earth is done and tomorrow never
comes, I'll be there.
When I have traveled the country and seen all I want
to see and am as happy as I can be, I'll be there.
When I have raised my children and watched my
grandchildren grow, I'll be there.
When the Lord calls me to be with Him, I'll be there.

When I Bow My Head

When I bow my head tonight I pray to God my soul
to keep. Without God's help we would not all be safe
and right tonight. I pray to the Lord to wake
tomorrow, to have another day to love the Lord.
He is always in my heart and always on my mind.
I can't stop loving Him.

I Have Been Blessed

I have been blessed with all the things I have received.
My family is always in my heart and they are always on my mind.
Emotions, emotions, so many emotions.
I have been blessed with a great church family.
They are always good to me.
I have been blessed with a great wife and home.
The Lord has blessed me and protected me so many times that I can't count them all.
I have really been blessed.

On My Mind

You are always on my mind. It is a song or a love story of someone special, like a girlfriend or a wife or Jesus.
Someone always there for us, watching over us.
Jesus is like the Marine Corp. He needs a few good men and He needs us now. Therefore, He is always on my mind.

Lifetime

Lifetime is the name of a table company.
But the Lord watches over us our whole lifetime.
He guides us, He protects us, and He cares for us our
whole lifetime.
If we are good Christians, we would honor and
worship and love the Lord our whole lifetime.

Lifetime II

Lifetime is a lot more than the name of a table
company.
Lifetime is the time you spend with your
grandparents, the time you spend with your mother
and father and your brothers and sisters.
They watch you grow and you watch them in their
lifetime.
Lifetime is the time we watch our children and
grandchildren grow.
They watch us in their lifetime.
And in our lifetime we love them all.

Don't Let Go

Don't let go of your faith in the Lord, because our faith helps us every day of our life.
Our faith makes tough jobs easier. It helps us get through bad days and days when we are sad.
It helps us get through days when we lose a loved one.
So don't let go, hang on.
Hang onto your faith.

Angels and Spirit Guides

We all have them and we all need them. They help us every day of our lives. They watch over us and protect us every minute of every day, 24-7.
They ride with us when we travel, whether it is in a car or bus or train or airplane. They go with us everywhere we go.
They are God's angels. God loves us and that is how He watches over us.

Christmas is just around the Corner

In this troubled world there are wars everywhere,
sickness, recession and unemployment.
People all over the world, let's get together.
Christmas is coming again.
We will be home for Christmas, so with Jesus' help
let's all pray for peace this year.
And the Lord will love us for ever and ever. Amen.

Love in your Heart

God puts love in your heart. For some people it takes
years to understand this or feel this.
It is a complicated thing, this feeling.
The feeling of understanding and how God works
and how He makes us feel about other people.
God tries to save the world one person at a time.
We have to understand that we are God's
children, and He loves each and everyone of us.
He forgives our sins and is always there to help us.
All we have to do is BELIEVE.

Our Saviors

They are always there to love me like they do, the wonder of them. Don't you know how much they love you? Don't you know how much they care? When you read the book "The Shack," you can see that all three of them love us so much. God, Jesus, and the Holy Spirit, all three of them are with us all the time. They are with us, in us, and around us all the time. They are our Saviors.

Joy In My Heart

There is so much joy in my heart because I know I'm free.
The love of Jesus has set me free.
The love of Jesus has made me happy.
I know Jesus is happy because He has set me free.
He put joy in my heart and that is what love is all about.

YOU ARE STILL THE ONE

You are still the one we love so very much.
You are still the one we are waiting for.
You are still the one we cherish and adore.
We are waiting for you, Jesus, to come back and
help us clean up this world that we have messed up
so badly.
We are waiting for you to come back with your
amazing grace, to save us from our sins.
You are still the one.

He Is Coming

I am listening for His footsteps.
I am waiting for His arrival. I know He is coming.
Coming to save all who believe in Him.
He is our Savior, God to be and I am waiting
patiently.
He will be coming soon, to touch us and make us
whole and take us home with Him.

YOU ARE ALWAYS ON MY MIND

Our Lord created the earth and everything in it.
He created spring with all the flowers, grass, trees,
butterflies, birds and large and small animals.
He created summer with green grass, growing fields
and warm weather.
He created fall with pretty colored leaves, ripe crops
with lots of food for all.
He created the winter with everything in hibernation
and clean white snow.
And so you see Lord, that is why You are always on
my mind.

There Comes a Time

There comes a time when we need all the help we
can get, when we hurt all over and our heart is very
sad.
There comes a time when we are lonely and blue.
There comes a time when we need someone to
believe in, to help us.
That is the time God gives us faith, hope, and love
and saves us.

We are a Spirit

We are a spirit in a body.
A body doesn't mean much, other than to make
another body.
A spirit is a part of us that goes to Heaven.
It stays with the Lord and our body goes into the
ground to turn into dust where it came from.
As my life is coming short, I do know where I am
going.
Maybe my spirit will find a new body someday.
And maybe my spirit, with a new body will do better
next time.

Understanding

Sometimes it is hard to understand the Bible.
Sometimes the scripture is very deep and hard for me
to understand the message.
The words seem to lead you in different ways.
The words try to lead us in the right way.
Sometimes it is hard to understand people. And
people wrote the Bible. Everybody thinks differently
and has different opinions.
Like in my writing, which way do I go with this? I
am trying to understand.

Special Moments

There are a lot of special moments that we all have in our lives, when we graduate, when we get married, the birth of our children and grandchildren and for us older ones, retirement. But for me that most special moment, was when I joined church and accepted God as my Savior. God gives me peace of mind and peace in my heart. He gave me faith, hope and love that I never had before.

Because of You

Because of You I travel on the short and narrow.
Because of You I am not afraid.
Because of You I have learned how to love and have faith and hope.
Because of You Lord, You have taught me so much.
Because of You, You have brought me from the wrong side of the tracks.
Because of You Lord, You have saved me.
I am not perfect but You have forgiven me.

Today is another Miracle

Today is the beginning of another one of God's miracles. God brings the dawn with soft light that hugs and warms the earth. God raises the sun with bright light and heat that warms the soil. By noon the sun is overhead with heat and light that will give you a fast suntan. The light is starting to fade by late afternoon with a cooling effect and the light is mortal. When evening comes the sun sets and the stars appear. Another one of God's miracles, day comes to an end.

A Temporary Home

This is our temporary home.
That is where we are right now.
We are here for a short time.
We are here for a short stop while on our way to heaven.
We are here to create a family, while on our way to be with our big family in heaven.
While we are here, we all have some pain. But in heaven there will be no more pain, in our full time home.

In God's Hands

We are all in God's hands.
Regardless of who we are.
Regardless of where we are.
Regardless of what we are or what color we are.
We are all God's children.
As we look up to the Heavens, someday we will all
go home in Heaven to be with our Lord.
He will look after us and take care of us.

Help me make it through the night

Help me make it through the night.
With all the pains that we have, old age, gout,
arthritis, and rheumatism, all the things we pay for
from all the good times of our youth.
Now that we are getting older we go to God for help.
He is always there with His love, hope, and faith.
There is nothing short of dying.
God helps me make it through the night.

You Are Never Alone

You are never alone regardless of where you are, or
who you are.
If you believe, then God is there with you.
He is blessing you and protecting you as you go
through life, through all kinds of dangers.
God puts us through tests.
As long as we believe and keep on believing and
don't give up, we will pass the test.

Only In America

Only in America do we have our dreams and the red,
white and blue flag.
We have our freedom of speech and religion.
There are so many countries that do not have the
freedom of religion.
If you go there and try to teach Christianity, they will
run you out.
Some countries believe in more than one god or they
worship idols or statues.
We believe in one God. He is so good to us and He
loves us more than anything in the world.

Searching

Searching for a four leaf clover,
Searching for a long happy life,
Searching for happiness in heaven,
Searching for a talk with God,
Searching for peace of mind.
I think at my old age,
I have finally found all of these by believing in the
Lord all mighty.
He has my mind and my soul.

Springtime

Springtime is when God works the hardest.
He puts in a lot of overtime, night and day, around
the clock.
He puts the buds on the trees to make beautiful
leaves.
He makes the grass grow a real pretty green.
He makes the garden seeds sprout.
He makes the corn seed grow to feed us.
He makes the flowers grow with all the pretty colors,
shapes and kinds.
With all this power, He is one great God. And all His
love is for us.

We Have To Change Our Ways

We have to change our ways when the Lord says we should be faithful and truthful to everyone around us.
Jesus paid the ultimate price for sins just like our soldiers paid the ultimate price for our country.
We should change our ways to live up to what they died for.
We should be humbled and grateful that they did that for us.

It's Not What You Take

It's not what you take with you when you leave this world, it's what you leave behind.
We should leave behind a legacy of good things.
Like our love for our family, and memories of the good times together, hunting, fishing and traveling together.
We should have good times with our church family, where we worship together with the Lord.
We are all God's children and someday we will all be with Him in Heaven.

We have a friend in Jesus

God is real, how much more proof do you need.
There are clues all around us all year long.
Like babies being born and growing up, and all the
animals being born.
Like the forest and grass and flowers and gardens so
pretty to look at.
With the sunshine, rainbows, the pretty sky and the
moon so full and bright at night.
How much more proof do you need?

A Tribute to John Denver

After seeing and hearing James Garrett sing John
Denver's songs and telling about John Denver, what
an impressive man he was. John Denver wrote 147
songs, but he said he did not write anything. When
God sent a song his way, John just reached out and
grabbed the song as it came by.
John Denver had a gift. When God sent John wrote it
down. Most songs came to him in ten minutes. All
his songs told a beautiful story about home, country
and mountains. I am really a fan of John Denver and
I sure do wish that John was still around.

FATHERS' DAY

The love that fathers have for their children is
unconditional.
They are fathers always and forever.
They eat together, play together, and worship
together.
Their love for each other is deep and lasts forever.

Remember When

Remember when we were young.
Remember when we had good memories.
Remember when 30 was old.
Remember when our Lord was watching over us and
He is still watching over us now.
I remember when I didn't understand what Jesus,
God and the Holy Spirit meant.
But now they mean more to me every day.

Grateful

To be grateful to be alive, to be thankful to be able to see.
When we meet someone, to be grateful to be able to see them. To be thankful when love finds a way to your heart.
To accept all of God's grace, like faith, hope and love.
To appreciate being alive and able to get out of bed in the morning, and walking and talking and just breathing.
To be thankful for the second chance God gave me in 1984.
I do thank Him a million times over.

Satisfied

Are you satisfied with yourself?
Are you satisfied with your income, your home, your way of life, your car, your wife?
If you are satisfied, then you are happy.
God gives you faith, hope and love.
That makes you full and happy.
That makes you satisfied.

My Favorite Song

Amazing Grace how sweet the sound that saved a wretch like me. God did save me in 1984. He saved me and gave me a second chance on life and He forgave my sins.

I once was lost but now I'm found, blind but now I see.

I was lost for many years, but now I do believe and I do understand. He made me see. How precious is God's grace that appeared the hour I first believed. And grace will lead you home.

Islands in the Stream

God gives us His love and what we do with His love is important.
Each and every person handles it differently.
We live differently and we love differently.
We are all like islands in the stream.
The stream is love.
We all should use this love to the utmost in our lives.

Have You Forgotten

Have you forgotten about God and country?
About the stars and stripes and eagles fly.
Have you forgotten about your pride of where you
are from and where you live?
Have you forgotten about how the Lord watches
over us and protects us?
Today is May 31, 2010 and I just marched in the
Memorial Day parade in Scio.
What an honor it is to march with all the military
men.
It feels really good.
I have not forgotten 9/11.
Where were you on that day?
Have you forgotten?

Need

If you need help, God will help you.
If you need comfort, then God will come and
comfort you.
If you need support, then God will support you.
If you need love, then God will come and love you.
If you need forgiveness, then God will forgive you.
All we have to do is ask and God will answer.

SATISFIED

Close your eyes and open your heart and you will feel it.
It's called satisfied.
The feeling you get when you have Jesus in your heart.
He gives you the feeling of faith, hope, love, and comfort to get you through each and every day.

I'm Carrying Your Love with Me

I am carrying your love with me, no matter where I go or how I get there.
I am not carrying your love in a suitcase or in a bag.
I am carrying your love in my heart.
I am carrying your love as proud as I can be.
It is a great honor to carry God's love all over and all the time.
He has a lot of love for His people. It is not heavy, but it sure is a strong love.

I Have a Friend in Jesus

I have a friend in Jesus. He has two favorite sayings, I forgive you, and God bless you and they mean so much to all of us.
Glory, Glory, Halleluiah. Christ died to make us holy and save us.
I wish we all would live up to Jesus' sayings.
Amen and Amen.

We Need To Pray

We need to pray for so many things.
We need to pray for the wars to stop and have peace on earth.
We need to pray for jobs for the people.
We need to pray for the recession to be over and the country to get back on our feet.
We need to pray for all the hungry people of the world and there are a lot of them right here in the USA.
We need to pray for honest politicians to lead us and not rob us.
So you see Lord, we really need your help to answer our prayers. Amen and Amen.

IT'S LIKE A LOVE SONG

It's like a love song, the love that God has for us.
It feels so right and so good.
It carries such a beautiful tune.
It makes me melt in my tracks.
It is a tender tune and it makes tears and goose bumps.
It goes straight to the heart.
Thank you, Lord, from the bottom of my heart, for this feeling.

I Will Keep on Loving You

Oh Lord, I know You will keep on loving all of your people through good times and bad times, through thick and thin, through high times and low times.
I will keep on loving You Lord, all this time, too.
Unconditional love is what the Lord gives us. And unconditional love is what the Lord wants in return.

When your nights are dark and lonely

When your nights are dark and lonely and your
days are not much better, call on the
Lord for comfort and protection to help you
through these sad and lonely times.
Believing in the Lord is so helpful and
comforting to us.
He is always with us.

You Are One In A Million

You are the one in a million,
You are the one in a million for me.
In fact Lord, You are one in a billion for us all.
You love us and take care of us.
I don't know how you do it, Lord.
It must be a full-time job, watching over all of
us at the same time.
But I know that you do it every day.

YOU STILL HAVE A PLACE IN MY HEART

You still have a place in my heart.
Through all the years that I have known you
and all the ups and downs we went through,
and all the rough roads we have traveled, we
stuck together.
Just like we did when we were young.
Lord, You are my good friend, and You still
have a place in my heart.

GOD'S DOORS ARE ALWAYS OPEN

God's doors are always open.
They are open for everybody that wants to go
through.
It is a good place that we all should go.
Heaven is a wonderful place to call home, for
the love that is there and the Lord's love for
everybody.
By the time that I am old and gray, I will be
glad to go there and this feeling is gentle on
my mind.

I WILL FOLLOW HIM

I will follow Him.
Where He goes I will follow, follow Him.
There isn't an ocean to deep or a mountain too
high to keep me away.
I must follow Him. Ever since He touched my
hand I knew that near Him I always must be.
He is my destiny, He will always be my true
love.
From now until forever, I will follow Him.
No one speaks like Him, Jesus is King.

A JESUS DAY

I wake up in the morning with a feeling of
another Jesus day.
Someone to lean on, someone to depend on.
A gorgeous day with no clouds in the sky, a
light wind and just the right temperature all
day.
And to think that Jesus made that day, the
wonder of Him.

WHY AM I A GREETER?

Why am I a greeter at church?
Because everybody needs a warm welcome, a
big handshake, and a big hug and to be told
that they are missed and that God is glad to see
them every Sunday morning.
And that God loves them. At least once a
week, I am a greeter to try to cheer them up.

LIFE IS A GIFT

Life is a gift from God.
What we do with it is the 64-dollar question.
Some of us do not use it to the fullest that it
should be used.
I think that we should appreciate our gift of life
more than we do and we should thank God
every day for this wonderful gift.

I WILL SURVIVE

I will survive with God's help.
God gives us all healing, like when we lose a
loved one or parent.
God comforts us.
He gives us strength and love while we are
going through our time of mourning and
adjusting our loss.
With God's help we will survive.

SURVIVOR

Jesus is a survivor. He died on a cross, but He
is a survivor.
He was buried for three days, but He is a
survivor.
He now lives with God and He is a survivor.
He also survives in our mind and in our hearts.
And our soul will survive with Him when we
pass on.

IT SEEMS TO ME

It seems to me that this world is getting crazier every day.
With all kinds of world disasters, from floods, earthquakes, and bad storms everywhere in the world.
It seems to me that the only thing that makes sense is the Bible and believing in God.
I hope someday soon that Jesus will come and save all us believers and make the world right.
Amen.

The Greatest Man I ever knew

It took all He had to make us new.
He is our hero, our Lord and our friend.
He did more for us than we, all together, could ever repay or do for Him.
Jesus' light will keep on shining in our hearts and in our souls.

ONE FINE DAY

One fine day Jesus will come to save all the
believers and take us all to heaven.
That is the day so many people are waiting for and
are expecting.
But when this day will be, we do not know.
So all believers are patiently waiting with faith, hope
and love for our Creator.

ON THE OTHER SIDE

On the other side there is a place called heaven.
A place we will all meet.
A place we will all be family again.
A place where everything is peaceful and happy and
wonderful.
It's a place I want to be, and I hope to see you in
heaven.

HOME

I remember all the wonderful places I have lived.
1. The house where I was born.
2. The house trailer in Macedon.
3. The house on the hill in Richburg where my sons were born.
4. The big house on King St.
5. The little house I am in right now.
I know that God was with me all the time in my life.
What a wonderful memory. I am looking forward to my next and final home in heaven.

SACRED MOMENTS

A holy communion is when the bread is torn off the loaf and placed in a big basket and put under the cross. Each piece of bread is from each person who asks for forgiveness and or pardon or help. The bread is put into the basket and then placed under the cross.

A SILENT ANGEL

Jim and Jill Kelly should be very proud of their 8 year old son. Hunter never spoke a word, but he watched over his parents every day and is still watching over them. Hunter had the influence of an angel. Hunter saved their marriage. Hunter died of Krabbe Leukodystrophy at age 8, but his influence will always be with Jim and Jill Kelly.

MY LORD AND JESUS

You are my heart and my soul and my inspiration. When I get to where I am going, You will be there to guide me and watch over me.
You will walk with me and talk to me.
You will love me as you do everybody else that goes home to heaven, our full-time home.

THE PASSION

The passion that the disciples showed towards
Jesus is overwhelming.
The look on their faces almost brings tears to
my eyes.
The love they had for Jesus.
They would follow Jesus to the end of the
earth.
And that is what we should do.

THE SOUND OF SUNSHINE

The sound of sunshine coming down.
The sound of sunshine setting behind a hill.
You think it is going to collide, but it doesn't
hit the hill.
God makes all the noise of the sun rising and
setting.

A BELIEVER

Being a believer is not a weakness. It is a strength that we get from God. When I went on the "Walk to Emmaus" it made me a stronger believer in God. After the walk I felt like a weight had been lifted off my shoulders. I got a new feeling on life toward myself and other people.

THE SUBJECTS

The subjects that I write about, I put God in the picture.
Because God is the picture and God is the subject.
God is the Creator that makes the picture.
God should be in every subject because God made everything.

GRATITUDE

There are so many days that we don't have any
gratitude.
We all should wake up and give thanks to God
every day.
We should thank God for our lives, our food,
and our families.
We should thank God for His love.
Without God there would be nothing.
We should thank God for his Son, Jesus, who
died for us.

THE BONUS

In April 1984, I had an operation to remove a
Cancer tumor. I prayed to God to give me a
second chance in life. And God loved me
enough to give me that chance. Every day after
that day God gave me a bonus on life. Every
day I wake up in the morning and I thank God
for another bonus day.

I HAVE BEEN BLESSED

I need thee and I have been blessed.
I have received thee and I have been blessed.
I have been blessed with the "Walk to Emmaus."
With all the kinds of feelings that I received in the 72 hours that I was there.
I have been blessed with the feeling that I got on the fourth day, and it is still with me.
I have been blessed with love and compassion from God.
And I thank You, Lord from the bottom of my heart.

THE NOTE

Write this down, take a little note, we have to tell the world just how much the Lord loves us.
Let the note say how the Lord watches over us, protects us, guides us and He is always with us all the time.
His love for us is stronger than anybody alive and many times more perfect.

THE POWER OF LOVE

There is no greater power than the power of love.
It can reach everywhere, the power of love.
All we have to do is let it move us and let it get into our hearts.
The power of love is unpredictable, it can move mountains.
It can change people from bad to good.
If everybody had love in their hearts, there would be peace on earth today.

A MOTHER'S TOUCH

A mother's touch is like God's touch, or a touch that comes from God.
A mother is instructed to touch or love.
It is sent from God to her children or loved ones.
The touch, with very strong feelings is sent along and passed on from God to any person that she touches, with the love of God.

I AM A BELIEVER

I am a believer. No doubt in my mind.

I am a believer, with all the love that God has for us and all the signs and clues that God has put out there for us to see and feel every day.

I am a believer.

After a "Walk to Emmaus," and all the love and feelings that the people have for each other, it makes us all be a believer. We are all part of God's big picture.

I am a believer.

The people are coming along Father, they are starting to listen. They are starting to believe.

Voices of Angels

Jackie Evancho is 10 years old and from Pittsburgh, PA.
Jackie sang on "America Got Talent" last summer. Jackie has the voice of a thirty year old, and she sings opera. When she sings, it puts goose bumps on me and raises the hair on the back of my neck. She sings and I get tears in my eyes. Jackie has a new album called "Oh Holy Night." She really does have the voice of an angel. Jackie has a wonderful future. God really outdone Himself on this angel.

THE FACE OF JESUS

When I see your face there is not a thing that I would change. You are amazing just the way you are. You are strong. You are the face of love. You are the face of comfort. You are the face of a leader. You are the face of brotherhood. We all need you Jesus, to come and save this troubled world.

OPEN YOUR EYES

Open your eyes, open your heart, let the Lord come in and see you and hear you.
Raise your arms and praise Him.
Invite the Lord in.
Be glad for the Lord because the Lord is glad for you. He will praise you too.
He is listening for your prayers so He can help you.

THANKSGIVING

We have so much to be thankful for, our health, our family and friends, our home and the food on our table.
I just noticed the number on this
writing is 109. The same number of Jason Dunham's ship, DDG 109.
So we really do have a lot to be thankful for.
We are thankful for a marine that gave his life to save other marines in danger. Thank you God. Amen.

BLUE CHRISTMAS

It would be a blue Christmas without you
Lord.
You are always there for me.
Lord, You are the backbone of us Christians.
Lord, You are the super glue that holds us
together.
Lord, You are the most important person in the
world.
Lord, You give us so much comfort and joy.
So you see, it would really be a blue Christmas
without You.

WAKE UP

Wake up, the time has come for us all to
worship the Lord. Wake up, the time is near
when the Lord is coming to save us. Wake up
people, it will happen soon. Wake up, we must
learn that we must believe to be saved. So
wake up people, the time is near.

THE HANDS OF JESUS

As I look at the picture of Jesus in our church, He is holding a lamb in His hands. Jesus has very big hands.

They have to be big. The lamb represents His people and there are a lot of people in His hands.

These hands are kind, gentle, loving, and caring, but they are also very strong.

They are strong hands that are holding His people together.

The feeling that I get from this picture is heart-warming, just to know that He is there all the time, 24/7, for us.

Waiting

I have been waiting for You a long time. I have been waiting for You for over seventy one years. I have been waiting for You all my life. I have been waiting for You, Jesus, to return. All the Christians of the world have been waiting for Your return. We are all patiently waiting and waiting for You to return.

SNOW

Snow is one of God's most beautiful creations. It comes in second behind rainbows. When the snow falls it is wet and sticks to everything. It makes a winter wonderland. It covers everything with a bright whiteness that is postcard perfect. I was in the woods hunting the other day and I enjoyed the scenery more than the deer hunting. The scenery was outstanding. Thank you God, for your work.

CHRISTMAS

Christmas is the day our Lord Jesus was born, in a manger below the inn that was full.

He was born the poorest baby on earth, but Jesus became the King of Kings.

He is the most important person in the Bible.

He became the most worshiped man on earth.

Jesus did so many miracles and He did so much for His people.

Jesus even died for all of us.

He is always on my mind.

HOPE

We all should have a lot of hope, in many different ways. We have hope for the future as in everyday living. We have hope for our children when they grow up and get married. We have hope for our health, to live a long time. We have hope for our faith. We have hope that Jesus will come and forgive our sins and take us home when we pass on. You see Lord, we have a lot of hope in you.

TURNING THE CORNER

We have been doing foolish things for a long time. Now we should turn the corner and follow the Lord and do the right thing.
We should turn the corner and follow the Lord wherever He leads us. The Lord is a special person who can lead us in the right direction. So turn the corner and turn your life around. Let Jesus guide you and make you proud.

IF YOU COULD SEE ME NOW

If you could see me now, compared to what I was two years ago. You would be surprised at how much I have grown up in believing in the Lord. And how I would follow Him wherever He will lead me. I will do whatever He tells me to do because I know it is the right thing to do.

FAITHFUL

If everybody came around to it and was faithful, then we could change the world. But everybody has to do this to make it work. What does it matter whether God is black or white or red or yellow, man or woman? What does it matter? We are all God's children and we are all different colors. What does it matter as long as we are all faithful? Amen and Amen.

I BELIEVE IN YOU

I believe in you, you have saved me from
being blue.

The Lord came with the sun, there was a job to
be done.

I am on my knees for You, I am praying for
your grace.

Now better days are here again, the Lord has
forgiven my sin.

He has the whole world in his hands,

And He has the power to forgive us all.

All we have to do is ask Him and

He will forgive our sins.

HE DOES IT ALL

If you believe, then the Lord will not pass you by. If you pray, He will answer. If you ask, you will receive. If you love the Lord, He will love you twice as much. If you need forgiveness, the Lord will forgive you. If you need a blessing the Lord will bless you. If you need a big brother, then the Lord will be that too. He is the man, like a one-man army. He does it all.

OUR LIVES

Our lives are like a very weedy garden, a mess. We have thorns, poison weeds, vines, stick tights, burdocks and ragweed that crowds out the vegetables and flowers and good things in life.
We all need to clean up the mess in our lives, so the good things can grow.
We need to bring out the good things in our lives.
We need help from the Lord to clean up our mess.

THE ONLY ONE

The Only One in heaven with scars is Jesus. The people put those scars on Him when they crucified Him. But Jesus forgave them. In heaven there is no more pain. God forgives all and takes all our pains away. No matter what our sin, God will forgive us if we ask for forgiveness.

GOD'S LOVE

You have to open up your heart and let the Lord's love come in.
The Lord has a lot of love to give to all of us. The love from God cannot come in to our hearts unless we open our hearts and accept this love.
We should be glad to receive it.
The Lord loves all He created, the birds, the fish, the earth and his people.
We should all love the Lord.

REAL

Life is for real. Wake up people. God is for real. Wake up people, death is for real. So wake up people they all go together, life, death and God. We have to get back to reality and live our lives believing in God, and then we will go to heaven when we die. When we go to heaven we will live forever with the Lord.

WATER

In the book "The Shack", Mack walked on water with Jesus. To walk on water is one unbelievable thought. But to walk on water with the Lord is mind-boggling. What a high honor this must have been for Mack. What a feeling of trust and faithfulness Mack had to have to do this miracle. And it is a miracle to do this. It sure would be something great if it happened to us.

STAND UP

Would you stand up for the Lord?
Stand up and praise the Lord.
Stand up and love the Lord.
He loves us, so we should stand up and love
Him, stand up and worship Him, stand up and
show the Lord how you feel.
The Lord is watching you.
There should be something more we can do for
the Lord.
Stand up.

YOU AND I

You and I, together with the Lord, forever.
God has been good to me. If I die tomorrow, I
have been really blessed. We do not appreciate
the blessings of life day after day. The moral of
the story is the Lord and being with Him. You
and I, all of us with the Lord, together.

THE GREAT MYSTERY

To solve the great mystery we all have to read the Bible, have a lot of Bible studies. We have to get other peoples' thoughts on what the Bible is trying to tell us about God. We should go on the "Walk to Emmaus" and give our full attention to God for the 3 days. Then we will just begin to solve the great mystery that God has for us. We should all be fishers of men and think the way Jesus did when He was recruiting the disciples to follow Him. When we almost figure out the mystery it is almost time for us to go spend time with the Lord. On the road home we learn just how much the Lord really loves us.

NUMBERS

If Jesus had a number, what would it be? A lot of people would say His number would be 1. For He is number one, first and foremost. God's number one Son. But I think His number should be 24-7 for the full time love that God and Jesus gives to all of us.

It Is Wonderful

It is wonderful to be caught up in this moment
of your life when time and age and maturity
come together with knowledge and common
sense.
Mixed together it all boils down to our
faith, knowledge and understanding of the
Bible.
Through Bible study, Walk to Emmaus, and
church, we should learn to voluntarily give
our life and soul and love to Jesus.

THIS BIG

Jesus loves us this big with his outstretched
arms, as far as He can reach. He loves us this
big. He reaches out his heart to us, 24-7, every
day, all year long. He is there for us.
Halleluiah!! His love is like a continuous love
song. It would be a great thing if we could
return this love half as much as He gives to us.
The present is a present from Him.

WALKING

The other day I was walking and picking up cans along Rt. 417 between Allentown and Bolivar. I was walking in the woods, the temperature was 80 and I had been walking for more than an hour.

I was getting very thirsty.

There was a little stream down off the road, so I went down there to get a drink of water.

I walked down and three steps in front of me was something orange colored. I thought at first it was a fox or a cat. But it was God's most beautiful little creature. It was a baby fawn. I had never found one like this before.

I stood still and the fawn never moved. I could see it breathing and its eyes gave me a God wink. I was amazed.

I backed up and thanked God for what I had experienced.

THE FIRST THING

You are the first thing that I think of every morning. You are the last thing I think of at night. All day long I think of You. When I am in trouble and I need help I think of You. You answer my prayers and get me through the day. Lord, You are the Savior that a true Christian has, and You are there to save me.

HE IS COMING

We should be loving God and loving each other. He holds my hand. He leads me. We should trust Him. He looks over us and guides us each day. We should not worry about tomorrow because God will watch over us then, too. He is always there always with love, grace and patience. Ready or not, Jesus is coming.

LIFE IS A GIFT

When we get a second chance on life, and life is a real gift, we should make the best of it.

Use it to the up most and enjoy every moment of life.

We should enjoy life every moment of every day.

We should thank the Lord for the gift of life.

We should thank the Lord for time with family.

We should thank Him for all He has done for us and all the love He gives us every day.

Because life is a gift.

HANDS UP

Hold your hands up to the Lord. Praise the Lord because He is watching us. Praise Him because He should come first in our lives. He should be the most important person in our lives. He is Joseph and Mary's boy. So praise Him, praise Him. We all need Him so much. I wish everybody could get the message of what we need to do. We want to see the glory of His grace. So praise Him.

ONCE UPON A TIME

In the beginning there was God. After all this time and all these years there is still God.
I believe He did it all.
From the beginning to today, He is still doing it all. Everywhere you look and everywhere you go, He is there.
He is watching over us all the time. To know Him is to Love Him.

THE CHURCH

The church is the house of God. It is a sacred, holy place where we worship. When I am a greeter, I believe that I should greet everybody that comes through the door equally, whether they are young or old, male or female and whatever color their skin. People come to church for faith, hope and love. The congregation should be greeted with the warmth and love that comes from God. This is what we try to do, with a handshake, a hug, a smile and a "Glad to see you," to everybody that comes through the door.

STILL

I will always love you Lord, still. Always and forever still, long and forever still. What a way to end a day, a minute, a year with the word still. Oh, what a feeling, like the "Walk to Emmaus" with the Lord still in my heart. After all this time, still on my mind. I am stuck on you, still. I love you, still.

GOD'S LOVE

God needs our love right now. He needs more than promises, He needs results.
He gives us his love all the time.
We need to give our love back. Life is not a one way street.
We should wake up and realize this. To receive love you need to give love.
We should pay attention and do the right thing, and pay back love.

ONE MORE CHANCE

Give me one more chance, when the time is right.
Just like the chance you gave me before.
Give me one more chance, Lord, just like you did in 84.
We all need one more chance, and we will make you proud.
We will love You Lord, for one more chance.
So shine a light on all of us Lord.

YOU'VE GOT THAT ONE THING

You've got that one thing that we all need.
And you give that thing to all of us every day
and night. With God looking through your
eyes, Jesus, you have this thing.
You have God's love that we all need. God
gives this love and all his glory, to us all the
time. Amen.

HEALING LOVE

We all have heard of parking in the
moonlight. What is wrong with parking in
the sunlight? At high noon on a bright
sunny day, set in the sunshine with your
sweetheart. Put your arm around her and
feel the warmth of love. This is the warm
healing love of Jesus' arms around us. Try
it, and you will get the feeling.
Jesus is healing us and loving us.

GIVING BACK

The Lord is so great and so big-hearted
for us all the time.
He does so many great things for us.
We should all give back, and give thanks
and give our love to the Lord.
He doesn't falter.
He doesn't wait.
He doesn't hesitate.
He is there just for us.
If we give back 24 hours a day, we would
still come up short.
So let's all try to give our love back to the
Lord.
Because He is so great and He is a keeper.
The Whitney Houston song, "I Will
Always Love You" should be God's song.

COMMITMENT

When I was baptized, to me it was a beginning to believe in God and what He is all about.

Whether you are 2 or 92 it is a commitment to God.

Communion and Ash Wednesday are a renewal or reminder or update of our commitment in our spiritual belief in God.

They all make a covenant with God.

This we all renew every week by going to the house of the Lord, so we do not forget God and keep Him fresh in our minds.

It's like a reminder to us, like a love song we should sing from our heart.

HE TOUCHED ME

I was walking with Jesus the other day and His footsteps were with me all the way. There are things we all pray for. We all pray for guidance from above. The hand of Jesus touched me. He touched me and made me whole. Just like on the walk to Emmaus. He touched me. He gave me that wonderful feeling, and made me whole.

MY PRAYER

I pray for a new day. I pray in the morning for safe travel.
I pray at noontime for our good friends and nice people.
I pray in the afternoon for hurt or death in the family members on our prayer chain.
I pray in the evening for our own hurts and pain and health.
So you see Lord we need your help 24 hours a day.

SEARCHING

Did you ever reach the rainbow's end?
Did you ever find the pot of gold?
I believe that it is there.
It's just like searching for religion, it's there.
God is there and He is worth more than the pot of gold.
God is our Savior. Search and you will find Him.
All we have to do is believe and search.
We love you God.

BELIEVE

Believe in yourself.
Believe in what you are doing.
Believe in God, Jesus, and the Holy Spirit.
These are the three main things in our lives that we should believe in.
It is like faith, hope and love.
Believe in them.

LISTEN

Listen to God.
Listen to the Lord.
Listen to what God has to say.
Hear what God has to say.
Listen.
He gives you the message.
Listen.
Write this down, take a little note, and hear His good word.
Listen.
Listen to His Good Word that will make us happy.
Listen to His Good Word that will make us believers.
Listen.
We should all be believers in the Lord.
Listen.

I BELIEVE

I do know that the Lord believes in me.
But I don't know what the Lord sees in me.
I do know that the Lord loves me.
I do know that the Lord forgives me.
I do know that I am not perfect and I am sinful.
But the Lord forgives me and believes in me.

GROWING UP

A boy sits down and a man stands up to follow
Jesus.
So stand up to responsibility and follow Jesus.
Stand up so the Lord will forgive us our sins.
Stand up so the Lord can count on us to follow
Him.
Stand up and be a man.
It all comes from the heart.
And home is where your heart is.

WHERE YOU ARE GOING

We all come from heaven with God's good
grace and love.
But where we are going is up to us.
We alone make the decision whether we go
back to heaven or somewhere else.
I would rather go to heaven. Life is a choice
and I choose life.

A PRAYER CHAIN

A prayer chain is a chain of people praying for
a person that really needs help. At the head of
the chain is Jesus with all his power, love,
strength and prayer. This chain is unbeatable.
This chain can hold the world together, even
in an earthquake. This chain is more powerful
than a big bulldozer moving the earth. This
chain can mend and heal anybody and
everybody that needs it.

GOD'S LOVE

Your love keeps on lifting me higher and
higher.
Your love Lord, keeps on lifting me higher.
I was lost and now I have been found.
I have found your love and you lift me higher.
Every time I come to your house, Lord, you lift
me higher. I have been blind and now I can see
your love. Thank you and Glory Alleluia to
You.

WATCHING YOU

Everything you do, everywhere you go,
every minute of the day, He is watching
you. You cannot get away, you cannot
hide, you cannot fool Him. The Lord is
there watching you and judging you. For
your trip to heaven to be with Him, He is
watching you.

TAKE A HINT

I want to give you a hint, listen to what the good Lord has to say. Can you take a hint on the message that He is trying to tell us? The Lord is trying to give us a hint on how we should be good Christians. The Lord is telling us how we should live a good life. Can you take the hint? Can you get the Lord's message? Take the hint from the Lord and do the right thing.

JESUS

He lights up our world like nobody else can. He works endlessly with all his power, strength and love. He is there with his beacon of light to guide and light our way through life. Jesus is number one. He blows us all away with all His power. This makes me realize just how small I am in this world.

APPRECIATION

We just don't appreciate the world around us
that God has created.
Everything here is so beautiful and so
necessary to our lives.
Everything is not just pretty but necessary for
our lives.
We don't appreciate how God feels about us.
We are senseless about how much love God
has for us.
We just don't appreciate what He does for us,
or his power and strength.
We really should appreciate Him more.

LOVE

Do you want to know what love is? Do you
want to know what love feels like? God has
that love. God gives you that feeling of love.
All we have to do is open up our hearts and let
that loving feeling come in. So come on
people, let's open up our hearts and let God
give us His love.

HOMELAND

This is my homeland, the place I was born in. No matter where I go, it's in my soul. My feet may wander a thousand places, but my heart will bring me back home. Back to my home town where I belong, where I will be buried and turn back to dust. This is my homeland and I hope my spirit will be with God.

GOD'S LOVE

Do you know what and where the strongest love comes from? It comes from God. If we put together all the feelings and agape that we get from family, friends and neighbors, it would not match God's love for us. The thoughts and feelings I have at Christmas time, the magic of Christmas, I wish would last all year long. I pray for peace on earth and good will for men.

HERO

You are the wind beneath my wings. You are my hero.
You make me fly higher every day. And you make me fly longer and longer. You keep my soul alive and make me feel brighter and brighter. Dear God, you are my beautiful, wonderful hero. You carve a path in my life and make me whole.

BROKEN HEARTS

Our world has a broken heart right now.
Twenty little angels have broken wings and only You, Lord, and fix this.
Dear Lord, heal the 20 little angels' wings and make them fly again. Please Lord, we pray for healing of our broken hearts. Watch over our little angels. We will miss them and love them always.

HOPE

Our church preaches about faith, hope and love.

FAITH

F   Father, One and Only
A   always there with endless love
I   innocents
T   Trinity = Father + Son +Holy Spirit
H   hearts of flesh not of stone

HOPE

H   holy hearts
O   oath to obey
P   pray for others
E   endure life

REACHING OUT

To be a good Christian, we should all reach out and touch hands. Touching hands, touching you, touching me. Reach out with our love just like Jesus did. Jesus touched people and healed them. Ain't nothing like the real thing, so do the right thing.

VALUABLE

Our time on this earth is very valuable. We all should make our time here count and do the best we can.
We should leave a legacy to our children. Because…
Our walk in this world will pass, and only our walk with God will last.

IMPORTANT

It's important to me to be able to write these little thoughts when they come to me.
It's important to me to have God, Jesus and the Holy Spirit in my life.
It's important to have a loving family.
And it's important to me to have a loving church family.

SHARING GOD'S LOVE

We should share God's love with everyone we
know, and help them receive it.
There is a lot of God's love and more than
enough to go around for everyone.
God's love is not lost.
We the people are the ones that are lost.
So let's all share God's love.

YOU LIFT ME UP

You lift me up. You carry me. You give me
strength.
You give me the courage to go on.
Only you Lord, give me the power to go on
through all the dangers, toils and snares that
we have to face in life.
Thank you, Lord.

STILL

The Lord will love us still. No matter who we are, no matter what we do, He will love us still. He will forgive us if we ask for forgiveness. We could be bad or we could be good, we could be white or black, yellow or red, it doesn't matter. He will love us still because we are all God's children. And that is important to me.

JOYS AND CONCERNS

I had a lot of concerns in the first week of March 2013. On March 7, the aortic valve was replaced in my better half's heart. Ginny went through a lot. On the eve of the operation, I asked her if she was scared. She answered me, she had God and she was ready. Ever since that day she has been a joy to me with her strength and happy to be alive attitude. What a joy she is to me.

WATCHING YOU

The Lord is watching you all the time.
It doesn't matter who you are.
It doesn't matter where you are.
It doesn't matter what time of day it is.
And it doesn't matter what you are saying.
The Lord is listening and watching you all the time.
The Lord is watching over us.

IF I DIDN'T HAVE YOU

This life would do me in, if I didn't have You Lord.
You are my rock, my strength, my support and my love.
I would not amount to anything, if I didn't have You Lord.
You helped in so many different prayers.
You are more than a big brother, with your hands helping me every day of my life. If I didn't have You, I would be nothing.

I HAVE A DREAM

I have a dream that I will make it someday.
We all should have this dream.
All of us together should have this same
dream.
The dream is, if we live right, be true to God,
do the right things, believe, trust, have faith,
hope and love, then we will be with the Lord
for eternity.

MY GIRL

You are the sunshine on a cloudy day.
You are there with smiles, laughter and
happiness.
You are my partner, my helper and my best
friend.
God sent me Ginny, for she is my soul mate.
She is a keeper. Thank you God for my girl.
Thoughts and love from my heart.

THE MESSAGE

God gives a message to your heart. We all
should take this message and praise Him for all
He does for us.
Praise Him and thank Him for all the
wonderful things He does every day.
Praise Him for all the things we don't even
think about, little and big things we overlook.
Praise Him for this message.

HOW MANY WAYS

We cannot count the many ways the Lord
loves us.
From the time we are conceived He knows and
loves us.
Through our growing years, all through our
adult years and our older years.
The Lord is with us and loves us.
He loves us every night and every day in every
way.

I THIRST FOR GOD

Some days my spiritual mind is overrun with
the hustle and bustle of the daily routine.
A busy life covers up every thought of God.
This should not happen to me but it does.
At my old age I should be thinking about when
can I go and meet with God.
I should be very thankful that God is still there
waiting for me to thank Him and worship Him.
Because I do thirst for God.

THE GIFT

It's not what you give after we die.
It is the gift we give while we are still
alive.
Day by day, the generosity we have
toward God.
Because God gives us gifts every day of
our lives.
The gift from God.

DRIFTING

Are we drifting away from religion and God?
Is the whole country this way?
Are we getting beyond the reach of God?
I hope not. I hope we are reachable so we can all be saved.
I hope we stay in God's vision and keep from drifting away from our Savior. I want to stay within God's reach.

LORD

You raise me up to more than I can be.
You are my backbone when I am small and weak.
You are my Father when I am young and shy.
Lord, I know you are beautiful even though I cannot see you.
You give me strength whenever I need it.
All I have to do is pray for it.
You are my Lord. I believe in you.

BELL

Ring the bell for the Lord.
I have the very good honor of ringing that bell
every week for the Lord.
Ring that bell hard and fast to tell the Lord that
we all want to come and worship Him.
Ring that bell hard and loud for the Lord, our
Savior.
We all should worship Him.

LET ME BE THERE

Let me be there in the morning, let me be there
in the night. Just let me be there. In the three
weeks that we traveled across country and saw
God's beautiful works of art.
It was a thrill just to be there.
I know God was there with us.
He protected us and gave us a safe trip, all
6960 miles of it.
Amen and He let me be there.

CHOICES

I had choices of which way to go in life.
Choices, choices, we all have choices on what
to do or not to do.
We have choices of which road to take in life,
the road to the left or the road to the right.
We should all make the right choice and follow
God.
To be honest, loving and forgiving and to
follow God should be the right choice in life.

IMPORTANT TO ME

It's not watching the Buffalo Bills play
football or watching Gun smoke or Bonanza
on TV. It is important to me to serve people in
need. Like being involved in church outreach
meals and Lions Club, coats for kids, money
for scholarships and eyeglasses.
We help the Lord by serving others.

YOU MAKE ME FEEL

Lord, You make me feel so good to be alive,
and to be able to travel and see this world that
you created.

What a wonderful trip we had, driving through
all the different sections of the country.

From flat lands to Salt Lake and Salt Dessert
and all the different mountains, flat top or
pointed.

We traveled along the Colorado River through
the canyons of time.

What a feeling this gave me, Lord.

DISTANCE

A lot of people keep the Lord at a distance.
I think this is wrong.
I think we all should keep the Lord close to us.
No matter where we are or have to travel or
how far we go, by car or foot, we need to keep
the Lord close.
We never know when we will need the Lord
for protection. I want Him to be there for me.

TAKE THIS ROAD

Take the road that leads us to good health and
happiness.
Take the road that leads us to forgiveness and loving.
This road is not on paper.
This road is the way we think of other people.
We are not perfect.
We should think of forgiveness and love for
everybody.
Take this road and we will feel good all over, inside
our minds and our hearts.

LOVING YOU

With all the love the Lord gives us every day,
every hour, every minute, wouldn't it be great
if we returned this love half of the time.
The Lord is more than a picture on a wall
or a name in a book. I will go to my grave
loving you Lord.

THIS LIFE

This life would kill me if I didn't have You.
That is how important You are to me.
Lord, You are it.
You are number one.
You are the super glue that holds me together.
Lord, You are the only thing that holds me up.
When I fall down you pick me up again.
Thank you so much, Lord.

SOMEDAY

Someday the man upstairs is coming to be with us. If Jesus doesn't get here before we die, then we should pray to join Him upstairs someday. Either way we should see Him someday. Someday we will all be together again.

WHO ARE YOU

Who are you, who am I?
In time we find these things out.
By the time we get old like me, we begin to
figure this out.
Take your burdens to the Lord and leave them
there.
That is what we have to do.
The Lord will help us with our burdens.
All we have to do is believe.
He will help us find ourselves and comfort us
and forgive our sins.

THIS IS MY DAY

This is my day with God. It could be any day
or every day of the week.
This is my day that God watches over me and
protects me from the evil one.
This is my day when God loves me and
picks me up when I fall.
He encourages me to keep going.
This is my special day.

OFFER

God has so much to offer.
It would take all day to list the things He has to offer.
From his everlasting love, to his army of angels.
 He is always there with His offerings.

FRIENDS

We all have and need friends and neighbors.
They all make our days enjoyable and meaningful.
Sometimes these friends come and go.
We then meet and make new friends to add to our lives.
The best friend of all is God.
He sticks with us all our lifetime.
He never leaves us for any reason.
He is there for life, with love and deep affection.

ETERNAL LIFE

Eternal life is God's gift to us. This life is our gift to God. We are supposed to live a life that is pleasing to God, with eternal love for God, because God has eternal love for us. Amazing grace, how sweet the sound that saved a wretch like me.

THE CROSS AROUND MY NECK

What does the cross around my neck mean? To me it means a true Christian, a believer in God and Jesus. It means that Jesus died to save me from my sins. It means that I am not afraid to die because I know that I am saved. It means to me that I am on my way to spend time with God and Jesus. They gave me faith, bravery, strength and courage for my future.

GIVING BACK

We should care enough to give back.
We should be humble and grateful for all we
have.
We should give back to God for what He has
given us.
God gives us many blessings. God gives us
angels for protection and fills our hearts with
love.

DATE

I would like to think very much and very
seriously that I have a future date with the one
and only God.
I am not going to wish that this date is near.
But someday it will happen.
I am preparing for this date in my mind, and
the way I act toward His people.
It is called love thy neighbor.

113

THE IVITATION

We have to invite Jesus to come into our lives.
We have to welcome Jesus with open arms.
Then we will live forever with Him in Heaven.
We invite Him by prayer and talking to Him
and letting Him know what is in our hearts.
God wants to hear directly from us.
We have to be genuine and devoted with our
requests.
God listens but we do not.

HOLD ON

I look at You Lord and You tell me to hold on.
Hold on to our faith.
Hold on to our compassion.
Hold on to our love for God.
Hold on to our God, the only true God.
Hold on and cherish Him.
If you believe it, now prove it.

LEAN ON

We all need someone to lean on.
God is always there to lean on.
God is so strong that we can all lean on Him at
the same time.
He will hold us up so we can face
another day.

COMFORTING

People have told me that my thoughts and
writings were comforting to them.
I think the most comforting thing, is
that God is there with us all the time.
God gives us comfort when we need it most.
All we have to do is pray and believe in God
and the comforting feeling will be there for us.

I AM

I am but a drop of water in the ocean.
I am but a grain of sand on the beaches of
the world.
I am but a pebble on the road.
And yet God loves me, comforts me and
protects me.
God does this for everybody in the world, even
you.

COUNT ON

God is someone to count on. He is always
there for us.
God's Son Jesus is also there to count on.
You can always count on them.
We can all count on the amazing heights and
depths of God's love for us.

SACRIFICE

We should all think of others before we think
of ourselves.
We should sacrifice our time and money for
our families, friends and neighbors.
God sacrificed his One and Only Son for our
sins.
God sacrificed a lot for us.

INVISABLE

God is invisible but we all believe in Him. We
know that He is real and with us. God sends
his invisible angels to help and protect us from
danger. Some of God's angels are invisible but
some angels have been seen. They take the
form of people so that they can give directions
to us and help us and lead us away from
danger.

HE TOUCHED ME

In my life time, I think the Lord has touched
me several times and in several different ways.
He touched me in spirit, He touched my heart
and He touched me with music.
He saved me many different times from danger
and with my health.
He touched me and made me a believer.

GOD'S HANDS

If you have problems or if you have fears, put
it in God's hands.
If you have weaknesses or troubles, put them
in God's hands.
If you have doubts about anything, let God
help you.
He is there.
Put it in God's hands.

SO SMALL

Sometimes I feel so small because God is so big.
I know that I am not perfect, but I know that God is perfect.
God loves me anyway and forgives my sins.
God is everywhere and does everything for me.

BEING A GREETER

Everybody brings love to church.
As a greeter, I can feel this.
I can feel this in their handshake or in a hug.
This love fills the church.
Each Sunday it is there because we have a loving church.
This is a very good feeling.
This feeling is like the walk to Emmaus.

COMPANY IS COMING

We have company coming. We have been waiting a long time for Jesus. He is coming for us. I am looking forward to this event. I am looking forward to spending time with Him. He will come with love and passion. Jesus Spirit is lifting me higher and higher every day.

A COOL THING

This is a cool thing. Jesus is coming. He is coming to judge us. I hope we are ready. It is cool that Jesus has the power, and strength and everlasting love to do this. He will come to us when we least expect Him. So we better be ready and get our lives in order.

TRUE COLORS

What color is God?
From what I have seen and heard, He is pure white, because He is perfect and pure.
He is a perfect God.
He forgives our sins even knowing we are not perfect.
He tries to make us perfect.
If God didn't forgive our sins, heaven would be empty. What are your true colors?

GOD IS THERE

God is there for you and for me.
God is always there.
God never fails us.
God's love is so big it covers the world like a blanket.
Do you know my God?
Do you know his love and kindness?
Do you know his power?
My God is there for us always.

YOUR BURDENS

Take your burdens to the Lord and leave them there.
Trust in the Lord.
He will help you and your burdens will go away.
The Lord walks with you and talks with you and watches over you.
Your burdens big or small, He helps you with them all.

BLIND

I was blind but now I can see.
I was lost but now I have been found.
I was unsure but now I believe.
The Lord put his faith in me.
I was hurting and the Lord healed me.
I was weak and He made me strong.
Most of all He loves me.

HOW DO I LIVE

How do I live without you God?
How does anybody live without you God?
If we didn't have God we would not exist,
because He is everything.
Without God I would have to give up.
He is my strength. He is my backbone.

A HERO

We all need a hero.
One that leads us in everything we do.
We all need a hero every day that protects us
every time we drive down the road in our car.
We all have this hero in God.
He is our hero.

ONE MOMENT IN TIME

Give me one moment in time.
The time I need and want to be with the Lord.
This would be a precious moment.
This would be a moment that I have been
waiting a lifetime to see and feel.
I am looking forward to this moment, to be
with God.

WE ALL MATTER

According to the Lord we all matter.
We are God's children and we all matter to
Him.
We are important to Him, like our children
matter to us.
This is important to us and our world.

LOVE STARTS HERE

Love comes from God.
It goes to our heart and our heart passes it on to other people through a smell, a look, a touch, a handshake, a hug or a kiss.
Everybody says love starts at home or in church.
I know I can feel this love in our church and in my home.

LOVE DONE RIGHT

Love done right can change the world.
The love has to be pure, from God to your heart and from your heart to all.
Pure love does it all.
It has God's strength and grace and love.
Pure perfect love gives everybody hope that we all need every day.
Hope gives us peace and joy.

ONE

One love, one God, one Jesus, one life, one wife.
One, the most important number of all.
The first number of all the numbers and the strength of all.
One person, one God, one hope for all.

SPECIAL

God is so special, He means so much to me.
I'm God's roots.
He made me from dirt, He put breath in my lungs and blood in my veins.
He gave me a mind to think with.
I am not perfect but God is working on me every day.
God forgives my sins, and He loves me every day of my life.

THE BEST THINGS IN LIFE

Some of the best things in life are looking at God's creations. Traveling the world and seeing the seven wonders, or just looking out your window and watching the four seasons change. But believing in God is number one.

IMPORTANT

What is important to me?
Starting out in the morning with a smile, a laugh and a prayer with the one I love.
It is important to me to do simple things and eat simple food.
It is important to just watch the birds and animals in the yard.
There is a reason for all of this.
This is God's world and I want to be a part of it from morning till night.

GUILTY

At one time or another we are all guilty of not absorbing what is said, either in a talk or a sermon.

The words or subject goes over or through our head.

We are all guilty of not praising God enough for what He is doing or has done for us.

Praising God should be a full-time job.

Praise the Lord for creating an egg in the womb.

Praise the Lord for giving it life and making it grow.

Praise the Lord for breath when the baby is born.

Praise the Lord for watching over children as they are growing.

Praise the Lord for watching over all of us as we go through life, with angels for protection.

Praise the Lord for taking us home at the end of our lives.

PRAISE THE LORD!

LET IT GO

Let your love go for the Lord.
The Lord lets all His love go to us.
So let it go from us to the Lord.
Do you ever feel that we are doing the right thing?
Let it go, let it go, let our love go to the Lord.
Lay down your troubles, lay down your pain, pick up your heart and love.
Let it go to the Lord.

OUT OF CONTROL

Sometimes I am out of control and I am wild and wooly.
I speak when I should be silent and I but in when I should not talk.
But most of the time God keeps a short reign on me.
God loves me and watches over me and keeps me under control.

NOT MUCH TO WORK WITH

God didn't have much to work with when He found me.
But don't underestimate the power of God's love.
I am a work in progress.
I am not perfect but I am learning every day.
I know I have a long way to go.
But God does not give up, He just keeps working on me.

LOOK WITH YOUR HEART

God looks with his heart and so does Jesus.
They both look for the best is us.
So let's not disappoint them.
Show them what is in our hearts.
Prove to them that we are good.
Look with your heart for the best in other people.

TREASURE IN THE BIBLE

As a treasure I do not mean gold, silver or
jewels.
I do mean a treasure for your faith, in
believing, in hope and love.
A treasure book full of grace and forgiveness.
A treasure book full of history and true stories.
It is a treasure just to read this book.
Our Bible.

LISTEN TO YOUR HEART

When you sing the national anthem, listen to
what your heart says. When you sing
"Amazing Grace" your heart tells you a love
story.
When we sing a gospel song, it is amazing
what the heart can say.
It is important that we all listen to our heart,
our amazing heart.

WATCHING YOU

Every step you take, every time you move, every time you speak, the Lord is watching you. Everywhere you go, every time you goof, every time you're right or wrong, the Lord is watching you.

GIVING TO THE LORD

Thank you for giving to the Lord.
Thank you for all the time you have given to the Lord.
Thank you for all the praise and love you have given Him.
How great He is.
I am sure the Lord appreciates what we have given to Him.
We all should spend more time everyday giving to the Lord.

HERO

We don't need another hero. We have Jesus. In Jesus we already have the best hero that mankind has ever known. Jesus is so amazing. He is my one and only hero.

ONE G – FOUR Fs

God
Faith
Family
Friendship
Forever
We all want what we can't get. We should be happy with what we have. We have God, we have faith, we have family, and we have friendships, forever. Something told me deep down in my soul about God, He is number one with me.

PATCHES

Jesus gives us patches for our broken hearts.
When we are sad, down in the dumps,
depressed and low on love, leave it to Jesus.
Jesus will build up your spirit and raise us out
of the dumps.
He will raise us to happiness again.
Because Jesus patches our broken hearts.

FRIENDS

Remember friends are like stars, they are
always there, even in the daytime when we
can't see them.
Just like God.
He is always there, day or night.
We can't see Him but we can feel his presence
when He helps us with our daily burdens.
He helps us with faith, hope and love.

WHO DO YOU WELCOME

I welcome God into my home.
I welcome God's Son, Jesus into my home.
They are welcome to stay in my home forever.
I welcome them anytime, day or night.
Any day of the week, they are both welcome.

ONE PRAYER

One prayer can help us so much.
It has the power of many a man.
One prayer can help us in so many different
ways.
One prayer can relieve our minds and make a
tough job easier.
One prayer can save a life.
I believe in prayer.
I have seen it work.
One prayer can help you and me.
May I pray for you?

WHO ARE YOU

Do you know pain?
Do you have heart?
Do you have a generous heart?
Do you have feelings for the sick and poor?
Do you have love?
Then you are a good Christian with love for all.

JESUS TAKE THE WHEEL

I can't do this by myself.
I need your help.
So Jesus, lead me.
I need you Jesus to bring me home.
So Jesus, take the wheel and bring me home and stand by me.

TAKE IT ALL

God has so much love that He wants to give to
us, so take it all.
God has so much hope that is available,
so take it all.
And we should all thank God.

TONIGHT YOU ARE MINE

When I retire at night, I have the feeling that
You, Lord are with me.
I know Lord, that You will be there, to take
care of me.
To comfort me after a long grueling day.
You make me feel safe and comfortable for a
long night of rest.
You build me up for another hard ahead.

CLING

If we are going to cling to someone or
something, let it be God.
He will give you the strength and power and
will and faith to cling to Him.
All we have to do is believe.

GOD CARES

God cares about us all the time.
There would not be any hope of heaven if God
did not care.
God made heaven for us.
He really cares for us, day and night, 24/7.

DREAM

Did you ever have a dream of what Heaven is all about?
Did you read the book "Heaven is for Real" or see the movie?
Wow! It really seems real to me.
It seems like a very nice place to go as our last stop.
It is a place of peace and comfort.

A PICTURE

A picture is worth a thousand words but I think a few kind words is worth a picture.
God has a plan, He paints us a good picture and all we need is a few kind words between us to make a happy picture.

ONE FINE DAY

One fine day when I know that my days are over, I know Lord, that You will be there to take care of me.
You will comfort me, love me and lead me to heaven, to that glorious place with You.

WHEN YOU ARE DOWN

When you are down, all you have to do is pray, and God will be there, giving you a helping hand.
He will help us no matter what we need.
Day or night.

FEEL

You make me feel so good.
So full of spirit, so full of hope, so full of love
for my family and my church family.
I hope that feeling lasts forever.

A GIFT TO THE WORLD

Jesus was the best gift that the world will ever
get.
It would be great if He came back again.
We sure could use Him right now.
This world needs some help and straightening
out.

SEE YOU AGAIN

Lord, we see you in a sunset,
Lord, we see you in the seashore,
Lord, we see you in the sunrise,
Lord, we see you in the frost on the landscape.
Lord, we see you in a rainbow.
Lord, I am always looking forward to seeing
you again.

I STILL BELIEVE

After all these years on God's earth, and after
all the good and bad things that have come my
way, and all the good days and bad days, I
STILL BELIEVE.

REAL MEN LOVE JESUS

Real men love Jesus, real women and children
love Jesus, too.
After all, we are all real.
Jesus loves all of us regardless of our age or
the color of our skin.   Amen.
After all, life is real.

MY CHURCH

My church means so much to me.
Of course the church is only a building, but the
people in the building are the "church."
These people mean so much to me.
I love them all and they can't do anything
about it.

FLYING WITHOUT WINGS

When I did the walk to Emmaus, after all the
hours of talks and music and love that I was
exposed to, on the fourth day I got an
unexplainable feeling.
It was like flying without wings.
It was a feeling that I never had before in my
life and have never had again.
It was wonderful!!

ENJOY THE MOMENT

Today is the first day of the rest of your life, so
make the most of it.
Enjoy the moment.
Take in all the good things of life.
God wants you to enjoy life.
Have fun and enjoy the moment.
Every moment counts.

THE DAY I GO HOME

The day I go home will be a very special day.
My body will return to dust, but my soul will
be home with God and Jesus.

COME TO CHURCH

We come to church every week to feel the
spirit within these walls.
There is a lot of spirit and love in this church.
We all enjoy listening to our minister as she
preaches the good word.
She keeps us straight on the good path as a
follower of Jesus.

UNDER PRESSURE

There are times when we are all under pressure
and tension.
This is not good for our blood pressure or our
heart.
This could be from work or family problems.
With prayer we should let God help us solve
all our problems.
Take your problems to God.

I NEED THEE

I need Thee every hour.
I need Thee my Savior, all day and all night.
I need Thee all of the time.
All we have to do is believe.

IMPORTANT TO ME

Joey and Rory Feek are a Christian singing duo. They sang about things that were important to them, like seeing a sunset, having a cup of coffee, having a great day, being with family, watching the birds, and all the little things in life. These things are also important to me, like listening to "Amazing Grace."

Joey Feek passed away on Friday, March 4, 2016.
She will be missed.

TIME

If I could just turn back time, I would find a way to correct all the mistakes I made, and make them right, and ask for forgiveness. Thank you Lord, for forgiveness.

HEARTBROKEN

I am heartbroken for the direction that this
great country has been going.
It has been going away from religion and the
love that we used to hear.
I am heartbroken that Jesus has not come back
yet to straighten this world out.
We surely do need Him.

GOD KNOWS YOUR HEART

God raises up your heart and lifts is way up
high.
God doesn't let you down.
When your heart is up high, God will keep it
there, because He lives there and wants to keep
you with Him.

WALK ON

Walk on, open your heart and believe.
Believe with all your heart and walk on with
Jesus.
Walk on with the Lord.
He is our Savior and we need Him.

EYES

Look into Jesus' eyes, watch His eyes open up
the gates.
The gates to His heart, the gates to His love,
the gates to His home.
His eyes will open up the gates to heaven.

CREDIT

I enjoy writing, but I want all the credit to go
to God and His one and only Son, Jesus Christ,
who sacrificed His life for our sins.
They should get the credit because they give
me the words and I write them down.
They are so wonderful.

HUMBLE AND KIND

Always stay humble and kind.
Pray to the Lord and help the poor, feed the
hungry, and help the needy.
Always stay humble and kind.
Love your neighbor and the sick, do what is
right and always stay humble and kind.

PIECE BY PIECE

Piece by piece He created me.
Piece by piece He created my soul.
Piece by piece He saved me.
It just took a long time.

CREATION

We are all God's creation. We were created by
God. How great thou art. I think God did a
good job. All we have to do now is love our
creator and honor Him and love Him just like
He loves us. Need I say more?

WALK ALONE

When you believe and you pray every day, you will never walk alone. Jesus will always be there to walk with you, no matter where you are or where you travel. He will be with you to watch over you. It is like two sets of footprints in the sand, and when there is only one He is carrying you.

THAT MOMENT

The moment that we start to pray at our meals, the moment that we go to church and pray, the moment that we do away with the pressure of life and realize the mystery of God and accept Him as our Savior, that is a wonderful moment.

PRECIOUS LORD

Our Lord really is precious to us. He is so important to all of us. He is the rock at the corner of our church. He is the corner stone of our life, the strength we all need. He gives love to all of us. The precious Lord gives us strength to go on each and every day. All we have to do is believe in him.

IMPORTANT TO ME

Let God help us with our hopes and dreams.
Let God be there with us all the time.
God should be with us when we spend time with family and friends.
God is with us when we look at a rainbow or when we see frost on the trees and grass.
God is there all the time.
And that is important to me.

STAND BY YOUR GOD

Stand by your God, after all He stands by you every day.
Night and day He is there to look after you, protect you, and love you.
He is there for you because He is your Father and you are His child. This is a family thing, so stand by your God.

SHIPS AT SEA

God goes with you wherever you go, even on a ship at sea. The ship goes out and spends many days and nights at sea. Through calm or rough seas, whether the waves are three feet high or thirty feet high, God is still with us. Whether we are out to sea for one day or one month, He is with us always.

DOWN THE ROAD

I have traveled down this same road a thousand times, but the last time I realized all of God's creations. It's like I just woke up for the first time and realized what is around me, under me, and over me. It was amazing what I saw and felt. All we have to do is stop and smell the roses and we will be surprised.

WHEN I SEE YOU AGAIN

I got this feeling in my body, I got this feeling in my heart and it's a happy feeling. I got this feeling that I am going to see them again. I mean when I leave this world, I will see my family and friends again. We will all be together in heaven Amen.

INDEX

Made in the USA
Columbia, SC
18 September 2022

67201001R00095